R A C E

TO THE

STARTING LINE

succeed in college by leaving grades behind

PAWAN MURTHY

Purchase this book on **Amazon.com** or **PawanMurthy.com**.

To my loving wife Kim,
who supports all my endeavors. I am proud
to be the man I am now because of her.

*   *   *

Thank you to Shree and Padma Murthy and
Karen and Everett Dennison for supporting the
development of my first book. I also want to thank
my editor Mark Mackinder (author of How to Melt
Handcuffs*) for his time, wisdom and guidance.*

Contents

Whether you call it a "financial crisis" or a "recession," you can't help feeling that our world today sucks. Rampant greed, poor accountability, and bad judgment have put millions of people out of their homes or their jobs and have driven many companies into bankruptcy.

Needless to say the job market for college graduates over the next couple years will suck as well. The National Association of Colleges and Employers (NACE) reports that employers will hire 22% fewer graduates in 2009 than the previous year.

Sounds like doom and gloom? Sure, you can sulk about the horrible job market and lapse into a state of complacency.

Or you can do something about it. Companies are hiring less – but they are still hiring. The way I see it, someone has to get the job – might as well be you.

What doesn't get a lot of press is that employers are using their internship programs as a primary source of new hires. In fact, according to NACE, internship salaries are increasing by 4.9% when compared to 2007-2008 interns.

For these reasons and more, being proactive about your career while still in college is absolutely necessary. There are so many paths you can take, and researching them all is a daunting task. You'll also have to juggle your school work, maybe even a job for spending money, and - oh yeah - a social life.

However, the effort you put into finding your career is worth it. I truly believe you will find success when you find what you are passionate about. How do you do that? The obvious answers are trying different majors, applying for internships, networking with professionals, or researching co-op programs.

But I wrote this book to provide a more subtle answer: learn more about yourself *by thinking about what makes you* happy. *In the end, I believe that is what we're all searching for, and I know that you will find it.*

Pawan Murthy
April 22, 2009

1

"What does a bachelor's degree mean to an employer?"

Sounds like a simple question with a simple answer. Many students I speak to respond to this question with various statements:

> "A bachelor's degree shows your experience."
> "...shows accomplishment"
> "It lets companies know how smart you are."

The real answer is far more basic. Based on years of experience as an employer interviewing many candidates, as well as asking many friends who are heads of HR departments from companies large and small, I'm here to tell you the real answer:

A bachelor's degree tells an employer that you've learned *how to learn.*

That's it. That is what four to six years as an undergrad tells the working world.

Upset? Shocked? You shouldn't be. Just think about it. How much of what you learn - considering all the courses you take as an undergrad - will apply to your career? Most schools require a heck of a lot of so called "General Education Curriculum" (GEC) classes, such as history, physics, or another language. Do you honestly think knowing the date of the Magna Carta will be a question on any job interview? No. (It's 1215 A.D. by the way.) Even for careers that require higher degrees (like engineering, medicine, or law), undergraduate courses only prepare you for a big test and/or more schooling.

Regardless of your major, you'll be taught the true work-relevant skills either on the job (through work training), in an advanced degree (through grad school), or on your own (through your work experiences).

I'm not knocking college. In fact, in the following chapters,

I praise college as the shortest period in your life that rewards you with the most opportunities for success. Nor am I knocking all these "extra" courses that are unrelated to your major and seem to be a waste of time. In fact, my most memorable courses were Philosophy 101 and Introduction to Shakespeare – both GEC classes which had nothing to do with my Molecular Genetics degree.

What you need to realize is that your time as an undergrad will train you to consume a large amount of data and: demonstrate you've learned it (by mid-terms), formulate your own theories (by writing papers) or apply it in some way (by having laboratory classes). The skills required to analyze, formulate or apply what you learned are critical requirements for the jobs of the Real World.

Oh, please. I can hear you groaning through the page. I know, I said it: The Real World. It's not even in reference to the TV show.

There is a reason why your parents, professors, books like this and others call it the Real World. The Real World doesn't let you explore your career or life options with the same ease and relative lack of consequences as college. Why? The Real

World requires commitment to one or more of the following: to a job, to a mortgage, to a spouse, to your children, to Uncle Sam (taxes), to student loans or more. Think of college as the shallow end of the swimming pool where you can get used to the water, practice your strokes, and let go of the edge – all while knowing your feet can touch bottom any time.

It's true that your degree shows the world that you've learned how to learn. But the years in college are for you to expose yourself to new knowledge, explore vastly different career options, and more importantly, learn about yourself and what makes you happy.

RACE TO THE STARTING LINE

So how should this change your view of your college years? I want you to start thinking of graduation day not so much as a conclusion, but more as a *beginning* - which is the premise of this book and my message to you. College isn't a race where the fastest time wins. You aren't trying to set a speed record like Jesse Owens or Jackie Joyner Kersey. In fact, you should think of yourself as Jesse or Flo Jo waking up in the morning, eating their respective Wheaties and making their way to the race track. Think of college as a **race to the**

starting line. You should imagine your graduation day as the few tense moments when runners step into the starting blocks, waiting for the gun to fire – the moment your hand grasps that diploma.

Once the race begins, you will face a daunting question: Now what?

You can reach the starting line in many conditions.

> You can be tired and scared of what the race ahead will bring, unsure of how you'll fare against the competition… OR

> You can be burnt out from the rigorous course work and exams you endured, apathetic about what you want to do and resign yourself to going down a path you aren't sure of because it seems safe or popular (I call these "default options.")…OR

> You can be energetic, proud of what you accomplished both academically and personally as an undergrad and excited to pursue one of many options you've crafted for yourself.

It's a stupid question, but which of those scenarios would you like to describe how you feel on graduation day?

I've had many friends ask that very question as we walked to our commencement ceremony. "Well, I've got degree in Somethingology, but I'm not sure what I want to do now," my friend said to me. She had a 3.9/4.0 GPA, graduated with many scholastic accolades, but nothing much else. No life experiences such as volunteering, no work experiences through an internship, no connections to people in interested industries/careers, no clear definition of what she wanted. She couldn't help but feel the past four years were a waste of time and thousands of dollars.

As I said before, college (undergrad) is the perfect time to gain helpful life experiences and a network of people to find your career. But why do so many students in your situation squander these golden years of opportunity? Because they, like you, face a huge distraction that pulls you away from figuring out what you want to do in your career and meeting the cool people you need to get you there. It's a distraction that faces every college student – that is worsened by parents, pushed upon you by academic counselors, and reinforced by your professors. What is this horrible nuisance?

They're called grades.

THE TRUTH ABOUT GRADES AND THE REAL WORLD

Let's face it. You've been given a grade on everything you've done ever since you were picking your nose in kindergarten. How you color a picture, if you determined when the train will arrive at the station, why you thought *A Tale of Two Cities* was such an awesome book – all graded projects. Your GPA summed up your entire high school experience in one number – and this was what you showed to colleges. Now that you're in college, you are still threatened with the fear of failing grades – by your professors, academic counselors and most importantly, your peers. (Years after graduating, I would wake up in the middle of the night from a nightmare where I failed a class or forgot about an exam.)

The only benchmark of success you've ever known has been grades. However, in the Real World, there are no simple letters or numbers to determine success. I'm here to tell you that the grades you've received up to now and throughout college mean nothing in the Real World.

(Gasp! Shock! Horror!)

I can see your parents now – ready to write me a nasty e-mail, demanding I retract my blasphemous statement. But before they hit the "send" button – I want to explain.

True – if you want to pursue medical school, law school or any post secondary education, you'll need good grades as an undergrad to get in. But after you graduate with your MBA, PhD, or MD….

Grades still mean NOTHING. Ask your parents or other professional when the last time they were asked (as part of a serious conversation at work) what was their GPA in college. I bet it was never.

So, why do your schools, teachers, and parents stress about grades?

I'm sure if schools had unlimited money, and if teachers were paid like NFL players, each student would receive a personally tailored curriculum. Students would be subjectively measured by their ability to apply learned skills in their environment. But we all know most schools are under-funded (as are the teachers). In the Real World, grades are an efficient and empirical way to measure the effectiveness of teachers, which in turn helps the school attract smarter students, which helps drive more school funding, which attracts better teachers, which helps students get better grades…you get the picture. Some experts say our emphasis on grades makes students study just for the test while learning nothing. Others argue grades are needed so that students feel a sense of accomplishment. A simple book search on Amazon reveals myriad titles regarding our society's focus on grades. The good teachers know that grades are not always an indicator of applied knowledge. Unfortunately, they have to work with the system as best they can.

So what about your parents? It's obvious they care about you. They want to make sure you are taking college seriously. Grades are an easy way to see if you are. But if your parents are constantly on your case about grades, think of this: The world was a much different place if you graduated with a college degree 20 or 30 years ago. Fewer people went to a university, and the courses were more geared to their respective and traditional professions (accounting, engineering, dentistry). Graduating college back then almost guaranteed a job. Now, more people attend college and students have many more professions to choose from. Unfortunately, a college's curriculum can't keep up with the ever-changing pace of modern occupations such as IT or biotech. (I know we hardly used official text books in my college genetics classes. Each quarter the information would be outdated based on the newest research.) To make matters more complicated, students now compete with job applicants from all over the world, thanks to globalization. The need to differentiate yourself from the rest cannot be accomplished by just a high GPA and a bachelor's degree.

For all these reasons, you must realize the bigger picture. Your future is not solely determined by the letter you get on a test or a number you get at the end of a semester. Your future is not solely determined by a piece of paper you received from a school. Your future is determined by how you make the most of the resources you have at your fingertips and opportunities you create for yourself.

But as with anything in the Real World – things aren't always fair or logical. While I purport that grades mean nothing – I must also say that purposely slacking off is disastrous. A low GPA tells employers you have poor work ethics or are lazy. So to be successful, you have to learn how to win at these games. While in college, you've been posed a formidable challenge: do well in school but not at the cost of learning more about yourself and figuring out what you are passionate about in your career.

STOP FOCUSING ON GRADES AND START FOCUSING ON YOURSELF

It's worth repeating that your years in college are meant for academic *and* personal development. This is why it's imperative to realize that your time as an undergraduate is limited and you need to make the best of it. You'll still need to make decent grades, but you don't want school to consume your life so much that it cannibalizes your ability to do anything else. For example, if you're on a quarterly school system and are taking 21 credit hours of mostly honors courses, you probably won't have time for searching for an internship, networking with professionals in careers you're interested in, working part-time at a local startup company for a taste of real-world experience, or even just taking a course that has nothing to do with your major (e.g. "Glass Blowing 101" or "Intro to Chinese Art").

WARNING: What I'm about to say applies only to those who plan on working after their undergrad studies. If you are dead sure you want to go to grad school, vet school, med school, law school, or any degree immediately after undergrad, then SKIP THIS SECTION. Learn what you need to get into graduate school first. I won't be responsible for those of you who don't heed this warning and have your parents mad at you (and me) for doing what I'm about to say. OK? I warned you punks.

Assuming you aren't planning on post undergraduate studies (see the warning above), you should ask yourself, "What am I gaining from busting my hump with all these hard classes?" If you hesitate, even for a little, before answering that question, then I would recommend *taking fewer credits* or *taking easier classes*.

See? I warned you. Let the attack of letters from angry parents commence.

"What? Is he telling me to slack off? My parents would kill me." No. I'm not. Keep reading.

Granted, I'm sure your parents have certain expectations in your college career, regardless if they are footing your tuition bill. I'm not saying slack off – I'm saying let's not get carried away with grades ALONE. Reason with me on this.

I ask students, "Is there a significant difference between a 3.6 and a 4.0?" Not really. "Would a 4.0 get you $100,000 more a year than a 3.6?" Probably not. But then look at the kind of effort required to get a 4.0 vs. a 3.6. Huge. That's why few people get a 4.0 (and then get beat up for it, too).

All I ask is for you to spend as much time as you need on getting a good grade while having enough time to do what you want outside of school. If you're taking 21 hours of honors courses and have no time to hang out with friends (let alone try to network or work somewhere else for experience), you may want to take fewer hours per quarter or semester.

What's the rush? There's no hurry to graduate. Use your undergrad years to the fullest. Take five years if you need it. One extra year won't kill you, especially if you use it to find what you love, work at a company, gain real-world experience, or meet people that will propel your career. If you do any of those, I believe the expense of that extra year is worth it. The time invested will pay you back in spades.

So please don't buy into the artificial hype of grades pushed by your parents, your university or even your professors. While doing the best you can at school is important, it shouldn't eat into the time for the real reason you're in college – to take that first step in your career.

The focus should be on improving *you* - not your grades.

The following pages describe four important life lessons I have learned during my college years as well as during my fruitful professional life. I call these lessons "Pawanisms" – but you may call them your own if you like. I figure you've been reading up to this point, so why not read some more?

2

"You'll be hired not because of what you know but because you are liked."

Up until now, you've been told to be the best at anything you do – be it math, soccer, art, or basket weaving. The focus has been on gaining knowledge and increasing competency. But I'm here to tell you that your character, and whether people like you, is far more important to your future success than any medal you have won, any degree you have earned, or any accolade you have received. Skeptical?

PROOF: YOUR A**HOLE BOSS

Ever have a real jerk of a boss? Or a co-worker who's a complete idiot? You're probably wondering, "How the heck did these people get hired?" They obviously weren't given this position based on their intelligence or competency. They got the job because they were liked by the person who hired them. So while that moron boss or dim-witted co-worker may make your life miserable, he/she may look like the model employee in the eyes of *their* boss. I've seen this happen many times. There are people like this in every multi-billion dollar company all the way down to the student organizations on campus. You can't avoid this kind of illogical behavior. It stems from the fact that we are social creatures. We tend to gravitate towards people who are similar to us – or at least people we don't hate. Think of it as a defense mechanism that has remained with us since we were cave people swinging mastodon bones at each other. This is true in the business world (swinging bones and all) – and sometimes, it's not a bad thing.

There are many companies who had a fantastic idea, but the chemistry of the team was a reason for their failure. Egos, misunderstandings, jealousy, insecurity, short tempers, hidden agendas – these are ugly demons we all have inside us to varying degrees. Hiring people who get along or at least have agreeable personalities is a major factor for success in any organization. Conversely, the hiring of your idiot co-worker or boss says more about the person who hired *them* –

such as their lack of sensitivity when choosing team members who play nicely. A good boss understands these finer points and will look beyond your experience or knowledge during the interview process.

Which brings me to a very important topic: Why you didn't get hired.

UNSPOKEN REASONS WHY YOU WEREN'T HIRED

Nothing prepares you for the feeling you get when reading the letter or e-mail informing you that you've been turned down for a position. Sure, you'll feel like a complete loser. But to add insult to injury, their response is almost always impersonal, patronizing, and filled with corporate "our-lawyers-said-we-need-to-write-this-so-you-won't-sue-our-company" Human Resource Department horse manure. I bet it sounds something like this:

Dear Mr. Pawan Murthy,
We are delighted that you are interested in our company. We have been overwhelmed by the quality of qualified candidates who have reached out to us. At this time we unfortunately will not be considering your resume

further. We appreciate your time and wish you well on your job search.

(This is the actual response I received from a company.)

What should frustrate you the most about this message is that they leave out any constructive feedback about your application or, more importantly, the specific reasons why you weren't hired. You can't learn from this experience to improve yourself for the next time you apply. If you do receive a letter or e-mail like this, try to e-mail or call your contact at the company to thank them for the opportunity and ask why you were declined.

The most common reason they'll say is you weren't truly qualified for the position – which is completely valid. More than likely if you're starting your career, you don't have enough experience. There's nothing wrong with shooting for the stars, but you'll probably want to send most of your applications for jobs you think you have a shot at. I seriously doubt you'll apply for a Vice President of Marketing at Procter & Gamble when you just graduated with a B.S. in "b.s." (…also known as Marketing).

But let's say you found a job opening on a company's web

site that is the embodiment of *you*. They say they want the experience you've got. They say they want the hours you can work. Most importantly, the job responsibilities are everything you could possibly desire. How could you *not* get this job when they are calling you out by name as if it were your destiny?

But they decline you, and you are speechless. Everything seemed perfect, right? They liked your resume, and you nailed the interview. And now you are staring blankly at the standard issue "we-don't-want-to-hire-you-but-please-don't-sue-us" e-mail. What gives? Is there no justice in this world?!

Here are some reasons you didn't get the job that they'll never tell you – because if they did, you probably would sue them.

The job description was written poorly
Many times, the HR department of a large company asks the person who would have been your boss to write responsibilities and qualifications for the open position. Many times, your potential boss has little time and hocks it off to his/her admin or direct report. This person then takes his/her best crack at it – knowing they don't have

all the knowledge – and writes a poor job description. Another reason for an inaccurate job posting is the person hiring you has difficulty articulating what they need. They want to say, "We need a person who isn't an idiot, who doesn't mind menial tasks now and then, and is impressionable to do the job the way I want it done." Of course, the company's lawyers would crap their pants if they posted this, so HR changes it to something like "quick learner, good work ethic, and professional attitude." Pretty vague and sometimes misleading, isn't it? Poorly written job descriptions are common, especially for entry level positions.

You intimidated the interviewer

If you were ever the "smart one" in grade school that got picked on because you knew all the answers, you'll understand this. Though it sounds shallow, you may have been declined the job because the interviewer felt that you are smarter than them – and they didn't like it. Many times, you'll be interviewed by your potential boss as well as other team members. While your boss may think you're all that, another team member may be threatened – either by your accomplishments or your skills. This is especially true if you are the young one in the group.

When the boss asks his group what they thought about you, the intimidated member will air his/her grievances. This could just be enough to nix you.

Of course, they may be justified in their decision. Perhaps you came across too cocky. Trust me, I definitely get turned off by an arrogant applicant. Since team chemistry is important, a "know-it-all" attitude could be a reason to pass on your resume.

Regardless of the situation, don't discount the intimidation factor. Modify your behavior accordingly during the interview. We'll get into more about attitude a little later.

They just didn't like you
Or put another way, you didn't fit the team. Hey, it happens all the time. A good team – whether it's sports or business, consists of people who work well together for the good of the group. Your interviewer realized this and (fairly or unfairly) made a decision based on a gut feeling. If you get rejected and the real reason is because you didn't fit the team – be thankful. The last thing you want is a job with people who you don't get along with.

Of course, the interviewer probably didn't like you because you made a bad impression. You were late to the interview, you looked disheveled because you were arguing with your boyfriend/girlfriend late last night – whatever. First impressions go a long way. If something is amiss, then the job goes to the applicant who either was punctual or has no love life.

However, the antidote to a bad first impression is a referral. If you know someone who knows the interviewer, you may be saved by your common friend who can vouch for you. I'm not saying you'll get the job immediately – but you may just get a second chance. More about the power of your network later.

Now let's get back to the main point of this chapter: You'll be hired not because of what you know but because you are liked.

"But wait! You're saying skills don't matter at all?"

Yes. That's exactly what I'm saying.

But how, you ask?

You probably aren't going to apply for a cardiac surgeon's position if you majored in accounting. And if you want a career in fashion design, you probably won't consider interviewing for that paralegal job. So unless you love reading decline letters, 99% of the time you'll apply for jobs where your skills and experience meet the minimum requirements for that position. Given that – I can firmly say that your success is not at all dependent on your skills and *completely* dependent on if people like you. Let's take the most loathsome job in the world: the Presidency of the United States of America.

Depending on your political views, all presidents have done both harm and good to this country. However, the ultimate impact of a president is hard to objectively determine. In the business world, a CEO's success could at least be gauged by how much profit the company earned. The only barometer of success for a presidency that the layperson can use is how much Americans liked their president. Hear of "approval-ratings"? President George W. Bush ended up with very low approval ratings – and that overshadows the good things he did. President Bill Clinton had higher approval ratings – and that glazes over the bad things he did. Either way, the impact of a president's approval with voters is so great that it becomes part of history itself – and history can be cruel.

Certainly your entry level veterinary tech job doesn't have the weight of the Presidency, but it is *your* job and *your* career, so it should be important to you. Your attitude goes a long way. Am I starting to sound like your parents? Here's one of many times in your life where you'll smack your head and say, "Jeez…my parents were right after all…"

DO WHAT YOUR MAMA SAYS

"Be punctual, be courteous, wait your turn to speak." Sounds like your mom when you were in kindergarten, doesn't it? Your attitude can be the gateway for success or a constant stumbling block that only you can avoid. If there is one vice that I would guard against, it would be arrogance. I cannot stress enough the importance of humility.

As employers, we know you're smart – but we don't care. Your 4.0 GPA or your honors courses or your summa-cum-whatever don't mean much when you're making photo copies on the first day of your new job. Sure you could pout and grudgingly do your job half-assed – all the while complaining with a false sense of self-entitlement: "I didn't go through four years of college to end up sorting mail!"

Well, suck it up, and deal with it. Chances are the first few weeks of your first job out of college or an internship will be filled with menial tasks. Why? Because your boss doesn't know you other than a 30 minute interview and some words typed on a couple sheets of your resume. Ask your parents about their first job and they'll tell you horror stories. Accepting even mundane tasks with humility and finishing them on time with high quality starts **building your reputation**. Here's personal example:

When I owned a design firm, I hired a 3-D animator for one of our large clients. Based on his resume, this guy (we'll call him Dick) walked on water: worked at Pixar, graduated top of his class at a prestigious design school, tons of great work on his resume site, he was the *man*. I hired him on a Monday and fired him on Friday. Working with Dick was a not-yet-discovered form of medieval torture. Dick complained at every chance he had about the equipment, the job he was working on or how the client's requests were "stupid". Even the client didn't appreciate his rude comments during meetings. I fired him and a few weeks later hired a design student (we'll call her Quon) with a fraction of Dick's capabilities. But what Quon lacked in experience, she more than made up with a wonderful attitude. Quon was thankful for the job, made the clients feel good about the project and approached every challenge with a "how-can-I-solve-this" attitude rather than Dick's "I'm better than you," attitude. Despite Quon's inexperience compared to Dick, I referred Quon to other companies based on her charisma and personality. I told Dick to hit the road.

I've had employees who maintained remarkable attitudes no matter what dim-witted tasks I gave them. And to those people, my reward is more responsibility and challenging tasks that are real resume builders. Your attitude in the face of simplistic jobs will show you can handle more. It will also make your boss look like a hero for hiring you. He or she will be proud to talk about you to their peers or superiors – further increasing your good reputation and even your demand. Trust me – finding a hard working person with a great attitude is as rare and precious as gold. But *becoming* gold isn't difficult at all.

So please make your mama proud and listen to her advice. Your attitude will help mold your reputation. Your reputation will start opening more doors faster than your knowledge or experience alone.

3

"The people who know you are the Currency of Success"

Let's say you've got a great personality, and you're starting to build a "golden" reputation – great! It should be a simple task then to meet people and start developing your network. Your network is the single most important resource at your disposal – just like currency. The best part is – unlike currency – it never runs out, and it grows the more you use it.

Now, I used the term "currency" instead of "money" because "currency" denotes both quality and quantity. Having one thousand US dollars is different from having a thousand Mexican Pesos (at the time of writing $1 USD = about 200 Pesos). Similarly, a good working relationship with five people who are leaders in your industry is better than "kind-of" knowing 300 people from random walks of life.

The working world consists of humans (duh). Humans are social creatures (again, duh). Social creatures are, by definition, dependent on their relationships to others. Therefore, the working world is highly dependent on relationships – between client and vendor, employee to boss, or co-worker to co-worker. You can start cultivating relationships that can mold your career during your college years. Even if you're wondering, "Why would anyone want to know little old me? I haven't accomplished anything." Trust me. If you're a likeable person and produce quality work, many people will want to know you. You just have to give them the opportunity. You'll need to start *earning* your Currency.

Earn Your Currency

Why network? The obvious reasons are to get a job, to get a referral, to get a new client, or to get free stuff. Get, get, get. See a pattern here? Pretty selfish. Strong relationships are a two-way street. Therefore a more sophisticated approach is to determine what value you can add to your contacts in addition to what you specifically want from them.

Network with Purpose
You know that stereotypical image of the sleazy guy at the bar – the one who hits on every woman he sees with the same cheesy line?

"So, you come here often?"

Seems pretty foolish to apply in real life, doesn't it? Unfortunately, this is exactly what purposeless networking sounds like. There's no rhyme or reason to the kinds of people Mr. Sleaze talks to nor are there any common connections built. To avoid sounding like this guy (or the female equivalent), you must determine your purpose. Here are some examples:

- Learning more about the industry or company
- Seeking internship/job opportunities
- Sharing an idea
- Solving a problem either one of you have
- Sharing experiences in a common field
- Asking for an investment or sponsorship

As I said in the introduction to this chapter, good networking is about mutual benefit. If the other party believes you can add some value to their needs, you'll definitely get their attention. But don't fret if you haven't solved world hunger just yet. You'll be surprised how many professionals are open to talk to students who are merely interested in their field. (More on flattery later.)

Network with Focus

Let's say all you want is more information on a particular industry, say, zoology. Approaching a zoologist with the question, "Could you give me more information about zoology?" is too vague and unfocused. More than likely, the zoologist you just asked isn't the spokesperson for the entire zoological industry. So don't be disappointed if he/she simply replies, "Um…it's great!"

Start asking focused questions that you know your contact can answer readily, such as:

"Can you describe your role in your company?"
"What are you working on now?"
"What are common challenges you face in your job?"

Get the picture? Make it personal. You'll uncover a lot more about the actual day to day workings of your contact's profession from these questions. Be understanding if your contact can't go into great detail if the information is proprietary. He/she may also be bound by law or a code of ethics, as in the case of a lawyer or doctor.

Be Flattering and Courteous

We all love talking about ourselves – so use that to your advantage. As I mentioned before, most professionals have no problem speaking to students who are genuinely interested in what they have to say. And if you do meet the rare individual who couldn't be bothered – just move on. You probably are better off not talking to that loser anyway.

Make sure you are cognizant of your contact's time and other commitments. Some of the most exciting people to meet are also the busiest. So if they have to reschedule three times, it's not because they don't want to see you – it's because they have to prioritize. For them, meeting a potential client worth millions of dollars comes first. Meeting a college student comes, well, not first. Offer as many possible options for times and locations that are convenient for them. Most of all, be understanding, patient and gracious.

So now you've got a purpose, you've developed some good focused questions to ask, now what? How does one network? There's no right answer, but I will suggest a simple process that I call The EPCR Method.

THE EPCR METHOD

What does EPCR stand for? E-mail, Phone, Coffee, Recap. Let's break down each step here:

1. E is for E-mail
Send a brief e-mail to your contact to introduce yourself and explain why you want to get to know them. (Remember what I said about networking with Purpose?) E-mail is a non-intrusive but effective way to get the attention of most professionals. And when I say brief, I mean brief: no more than one short paragraph that fits on a "Crackberry" screen without scrolling. Here's an example:

Dear Samantha,

Hi! My name is Pawan Murthy, a sophomore at OSU. I'm very interested in pursuing a career in marketing. I received your contact information from Dr. Smith, my marketing professor. Would you have time for a 10 minute phone call next Monday at 3 p.m. so that I can introduce myself? I'd like to know more about what you do at your advertising agency. Your time is greatly appreciated.

Thanks,
Pawan

This e-mail is written in an informal voice. Being overly formal may put some people off – but still be respectful. I also suggest a specific time so your contact can reply with a quick "Yes, that works," or "No, but I have another time available." Since many people check their e-mail on their phone, it helps to write a message that requires a brief response.

If you can cite a referral (in this case Dr. Smith) you provide some validity which could increase the chances of a timely response. Also, I stated how brief my conversation will be based on my best guess. No harm done if your contact is OK with the chat going longer. At least you have set an expectation so they can add it to their schedule. I've also stated my intention of the conversation. This way, she can prepare for the call or direct me to someone more capable of answering my questions. Of course, this sample is quite generic – you make it your own based on the circumstances.

Finally, make sure you freakin' *spell check* and *proofread* your e-mail. Nothing screams, "Dude, I'm too immature to care!" louder than misspelled words, especially since every e-mail system known to Man has a spell-checker. And proofread it so it's intelligible. If you are unsure, have someone else look at it. You can find plenty of grammar web sites that describe common e-mail faux pas (e.g. "your" vs. "you're" or "they're vs. their"). If I'm contacting someone important for the first time, I read my e-mail 3 to 5 times to make sure I don't sound like an idiot. Some may call it obsessive, but I call it necessary. Once you hit "submit", it's too late. Your first impression (good or bad) is traveling at the speed of the Internet to your recipient.

If your contact accepts to talk with you, send a quick e-mail back confirming the time of the call. Most professionals understand that you're in school and have classes during the day. And though this sounds silly, make sure you are clear about who is calling who. This way, neither of you are getting the other person's busy signal.

All this work is to make sure your next step is as smooth and as predictable as possible: The phone call.

2. P is for Phone

Before you talk to your contact, do your homework by learning as much as you can about them. Research their background and their company/institution/organization. Your contact may have a profile on sites like LinkedIn, Plaxo or Facebook. Check them out and see if there's a common interest you share, or something else worthwhile. There's also this relatively unknown search engine you can use if those sites don't work. I think it's called Google? Maybe Googul? I'm not sure – but maybe you've heard of it. If they don't have a profile anywhere, their work should at least have a web site.

When you get your contact on the phone, ask if the planned time still works. You never know what kind of day they had. If they sound busy, offer to reschedule.

A phone call is a great way of sizing up your contact. You'll be able to quickly tell if this person is willing to help or isn't interested. You'll be able to understand if the information you are getting from this person is helpful – or not. Sometimes, you could be barking up the wrong tree – and this phone call can tell you many things.

After you feel you've got your questions answered (and assuming your contact doesn't need to leave early for any reason), thank them for their time.

At this point, you have a decision to make that is dependent on what you talked about. Perhaps you got all you needed and would like to continue keeping in touch – great. Or there's an event that your contact will attend that you've discussed would be good to go to (like a trade show or a conference).

Perhaps you've decided you want to meet in person to discuss something more – or to show them something. If you decide there's a good reason to meet, check out the next optional step.

3. C is for Coffee (optional)

There's a reason why coffee shops are so popular – even to those who don't drink lots of coffee (like me). They're comfortable, inviting, quick, and there's something for everyone. Visiting a coffee shop also fits in the daily routine of many people – so you aren't bothering them at the office. More importantly coffee is cheap – so even broke college students can afford to treat their contact. After all – it is their time you want.

Of course, it doesn't have to be at a coffee house. Perhaps they are gracious enough to invite you to their place of work. Even better! Heck, ask them if you could pick something up for them (like coffee).

When you do meet – just be the same gracious, humble, genuinely interested person who was on the phone. Be punctual and dress appropriately for the situation. Don't show up in ripped jeans and a t-shirt to a snooty law-firm. You make that judgment call.

If your schedule has changed and you can't make it – realize this as early as possible and call your contact, tell them the situation and ask if it's best to reschedule. Let them decide based on their needs.

When you do start talking – be courteous and don't waste their time. Ask your questions and shut up and listen. Bring a pad and something to write with, though I'd recommend *not* taking copious notes. This isn't a lecture – and there is no test. You don't take notes when you're with a friend, do you? The paper is there to write down additional names, phone numbers, or web addresses. Unless you're drawing a blueprint for a new widget their company can use, there is no need to capture every word like a stenographer in court. Also, lots of note-taking may make your contact uneasy.

4. R is for Recap

Whether you've met your contact face to face (as in step 3) or simply had a phone call (step 2), it doesn't hurt to close the loop with another e-mail. I recommend thanking them for their time and highlighting a few meaningful points you talked about. Perhaps there were some to-do's or other people your contact suggested you talk to. Of course, if the chat or meeting was completely worthless, just thank them for their time. No need to be fake, right?

The more purposeful and focused networking you do, the better you'll get at it. These steps will come naturally, and you'll probably have your own method that works best with your personality. Just remember the golden rule: "Do unto others as you would have them do unto you." Simply understand how you'd like to be treated and you'll get a good understanding of how to treat others.

Play the "Student Card"

As a college student, you have a powerful ticket into meeting various people. The mere fact you're a student gives you access to many people and companies. Why? Almost all professionals love talking to students. I personally don't know anyone in my network who does NOT want to talk to students. They all understand what it was like trying to figure out their career. If you show interest in what they are doing, all the better. (Remember what I said about flattery?)

Unfortunately, the power of playing "The Student Card" is surprisingly under-utilized. This is important because once you're out of college, you give up this power. Though not impossible, it's harder to network with other professionals when you're older – either because you don't have that "student sympathy" any more or because they'll think there is an ulterior motive – like you're trying to sell them something. Being young, bright-eyed and curious is a priceless asset. Make the most of it while you are a student.

4

"Do what you love, and the Wealth will follow."

There are plenty of careers that can just get you money. There are far fewer careers that can get you *contentment*. This feeling of satisfaction – where you do what you love and your job provides you the lifestyle you've always wanted is what I consider "Wealth." It's the feeling you get when you know you're making an impact on a facet of life that's dear to you. Earning money alone doesn't bring this kind of feeling. I know millionaires who are miserable – and people barely able to pay their rent who are perfectly content. Our time in this world is too short to be doing things that make us unhappy. For all the things in life where we don't have a choice, your career is one of the few major decisions you can control. So why not do something you love?

"CARE FOR A SLICE OF ANTHROPOLOGY?"

I probably don't have to tell you that your college years can be stressful. In addition to keeping up with school work and doing all the crap I've told you to do in this book, I bet there's an underlying feeling of uncertainty. Like you're forced to make a big decision about your career that will impact the rest of your life. Like you're Neo in *The Matrix*, deciding which pill to take. Or perhaps you feel you're being dangled off a bridge and forced to pick a career (with limited knowledge on that career) that could hurl you into a lifetime of misery.

Whatever the metaphor you want to use, you may feel it's a big decision you have to unfairly make without knowing all the facts. To make things worse, I bet you have friends who seem to know exactly what they want. Like your roommate who is triple majoring in architecture, medicine and flute so they can design ergonomically harmonious hospitals for injured flautists. Then you've got your parents' friends who keep bugging you with questions like, "So, what are you majoring in again?" or "What will you do after you graduate?" All you want to say is, "I don't know what I'm majoring in yet – like I told you the past 20 times you asked me that question." Sadly, you probably ask yourself this same question without a clear answer.

May I suggest changing the question? Perhaps the question should not be "What am I going to do?" Perhaps the question should be, "What would I like to try?" That sounds much friendlier and far less committed. It sounds like what the hostess would say at your local Chinese Buffet – which is exactly the way I want you to think about college: a buffet of career options. Sure, you've got to play the system and select a major – so do it. Take a good guess and select something. Or take a list of all majors offered at your school and start crossing off ones you don't like. Whatever is left – just make a choice. Really, no one is expecting you to stick with it. Sometimes, the hardest part of all this is just deciding on *something*.

So you've selected a major – great. You'll probably need to take a bunch of general education courses, right? You'll need to select those as well. Now let's focus on the fun stuff. Try some random courses. Extra points if they happen to be part of your major or your GEC's. If not – and it seems interesting – take the course! As I said before, some of my most memorable courses had nothing to do with my major: Philosophy and Intro to Shakespeare. Though I'm not a philosopher nor am I a Shakespearean expert, I was able to flex my creative muscles in ways that would never have been required in my genetics courses. I realized my brain craved some level of creativity. I realized also that I was good at things I never knew I was good at.

And that's the whole point of college: discovering your talents by trying new things. More importantly, you're introduced to different ways of thinking and are forced to use your brain differently. Either you'll hate it or you'll love it. Be brave in your class selection. Those classes are there for a reason, and you should make use of them. You (or someone close to you) is paying for college, so make the most it. Forcing your brain to work in strange ways helps determine what makes you happy. At the very least, you'll quickly know all the many things that you don't want to do.

DON'T BE AFRAID OF CHANGE

People far smarter and wiser than me have remarked on how money only buys you things, some of which can make you happy. But money cannot buy *contentment* – that is to say a sense of satisfaction you get when you are working towards something you love or truly believe.

This search can be confusing because as students, we're interested in many things but aren't sure if we want to make a career out of it. Here's a personal story.

For years and years I was a devoted musician. I studied piano under amazing teachers throughout high school and was certain music was my career. However, when I went to college, I realized I had many other interests. Additionally, music required a level of dedication and self sacrifice for a lifestyle that I didn't want. I also felt that music started to become a chore – and I feared that. I didn't want to end up hating music. It was a tough decision, but I realized that music will always remain a passionate hobby – but never my career.

So I thought my calling was genetics. I again was fortunate to study under wonderful researchers – all leaders in their fields. Though the work was interesting and ultimately can help humanity, I realized that wasn't for me either. I realized I wasn't able to use the creative side of my brain – which is important to me even today.

Though I was disappointed at the time, I look back on these experiences in music and genetics a major turning points. I realized identifying careers you *don't* want to do is a critical step in finding what you *want* to do.

While in college, my friends constantly poked fun at me since I kept moving from one major to the next. They said I was on the "12 year plan." For some reason changing majors or career decisions gets a bad rap with your college peers and parents. I'm not sure why, since, as I said before, that's what college is about. As long as you feel you've explored each of your choices enough to make a decision, I say switch as much as you want. Better to make these changes now than when you've got a job, a house, a car, kids, etc. Change is good - especially if you are learning from each experience. Change is essential to find what makes you happy – or what makes you fulfilled by doing what you love. This, my friends, is called finding your passion.

HOW TO FIND YOUR PASSION

Libraries have shelves filled with books that try to determine your future job. Some of these books contain tests that ask a series of questions about your personality, interests, or values. Based on a complex point system, these exercises calculate your exact future occupation: "You will be a fantastic phlebotomist." Seriously? I think these books are similar to scientists who claim they can predict earthquakes: good intentions but rarely accurate. Changes in the economy, market conditions and technology are just a few factors that can make an in-demand profession into a low-paying commodity.

While your job can change, your passions in life usually don't. Finding a career that brings you happiness usually means doing something you are passionate about. Finding your passion means being able to utilize skills which you are proud of having. While I can't promise I can help find your career, I'd like to propose a deceivingly simple exercise to help you find your passion. It all begins with your skills. I encourage you to put as much effort in this as you can. You only get out what you put in.

1. List all your skills
That's right, all of them. Sounds dumb, but just try it. Humor me. To help you out, divide your list into four categories:

- Skills you learned at work
- Skills you learned at school
- Skills you learned at home

- Skills you were born with

I'll give an example of each.

- Work skill: Fixing a computer (if you worked at an electronics store)
- School skills: Solving the quadratic equation
- Home skills: Your mom taught you how to make a mean apple pie
- Skill you were born with: Memorizing long lists of numbers

When I say list all skills, I mean EVERYTHING. Even skills that aren't necessarily nice – like "I can get men to do whatever I want," or "I'm a great liar."

The reason this step is surprisingly difficult is because the most important skills you possess are those you may not realize you have. For example, having perfect pitch (where you can tell the name of a musical note as soon as you hear it) may not be anything special to you. But your friends or family may think it's voodoo magic. Ask someone close to you to list a few skills they think you have. You may be surprised by what they tell you.

This takes a while so reserve a few days to put this together. Try not to read on to the next steps as your final answers may be skewed or biased. You should have at least 30 skills. If you can't get 30, you're either too hard on yourself, too lazy to think of any, or you're just a huge loser.

Go on, start your list and don't read ahead until you're finished!

2. Pick your Top 10 Coveted Skills

Assuming you have put much thought in building a long list of every possible skill you have then you can continue reading. Now I want you to select the 10 skills you covet the most. By covet, I mean you can't live without them. Or put another way, your happiness/quality of life would be drastically reduced if you were unable to use those skills.

For example, I love to play piano. If my hands were crushed by a crazy salt-water taffy puller accident (don't laugh – it does happen), which prevented me from playing piano again, I would be devastated. Perhaps you love to kayak but it became outlawed in the U.S. for some reason. Would you be devastated? If yes, then kayaking is a skill you covet.

Go through each skill you have listed. If you can't make a decision, then it's probably not very important to you. Only you can qualify what skills you covet the most. Make sure you've got at least 10. If you have fewer it may make the next step more difficult.

3. Fun or Career Skills?

Divide your skills into those that you think are purely recreational and those you think can be applied to a career. This is where the rubber hits the road. To some, skills like "great at kayaking" will probably be under the "Fun" category. But what if you want to be a kayak guide along the Colorado River in the Grand Canyon? Use your gut. If you truly can't decide – err on the side of "Career Skills." Wouldn't you rather have a job that requires you to do things you think are fun?

4. Review your Career Skills

Sit back and take a look at your Career Skills. This list is the result of a lot of introspection. No doubt, this isn't a complete list – nor is it written in stone. It is, however, a snapshot of

YOU at this moment. Can you make any observations of the Career Skills you established? For example, where do most of your Career Skills fall in the original four categories we started with? Do many Career Skills fall in the "skills you were born with" category? Also, what kinds of work have you done that have utilized some or all of these skills in the past? Were you happy/proud/fulfilled when you did?

Finding a career that utilizes these skills isn't easy. Think about the process of shopping for a car. Many people I know create a spreadsheet of features they "need-to-have" vs. those they "want-to-have". Some rank which options are most important to them and what they are willing to pay. Certainly, shoppers look at what each make and model offers before making a decision. We have no problem spending hours to find our perfect set of wheels. Shouldn't we be exerting a similar effort to find our perfect career?

With your list of Career Skills, at least now you have a basic set of requirements. You may not ever look at it again – but you may remember a few things you learned about yourself. Use this exercise to determine if you are happy in the career path you've chosen. If not, then you have motivation to change your path. As a college student, you have the power to make substantial changes in your career in a very short amount of time. So make the best of it. Take different classes from different majors, talk to professors, connect with professionals in your community, and most importantly – gain as much work experience in college as possible. In fact, I hope you are working on your next internship opportunities for the coming summer right now.

What's that you say? You've already submitted your resume to Procter & Gamble, General Electric and Hewlett-Packard? And it's been weeks without a word from any of them? The nerve! How dare they not pick you out of the 14,000 applications they get *per day.*

(Can you sense the sarcasm?)

Gravitating towards mega-corporations is easy because everyone knows them. Getting an internship there is difficult for the exact same reason. Unless you know the CEO or your resume claims you walk on water, your chances of getting hired are very slim. You should still apply since someone has to win it. However, I suggest opening your options to the thousands of small to mid-sized companies right in your community. You'll be surprised how desperately they need talented (and cheap) labor.

SMALL BUSINESSES, BIG EXPERIENCES

When I had my small design firm, we were very lucky to work on projects from well known and large companies. However, the most enjoyable, rewarding and exciting projects were with our startup and small businesses. Their needs were great yet their resources were limited. Finding the best solution given these tight restrictions led to some of our best work. Additionally, our services had such a positive impact on the day to day operations of these companies. In some cases, sales doubled or tripled, mostly due to our work. On the other hand, the projects we did for the big guys felt like a drop in the ocean – very little impact on the overall corporation.

I suggest working for small businesses because like my story above, the work you do will have a tremendous impact on the entire business, which will quickly increase your appreciation for responsibility. You'll quickly learn different aspects of a company – from finance to marketing – since employees of a small business have to wear many hats. They may not pay much (or at all), but what you get in knowledge and experience are well worth it.

Small companies or startups most likely won't show up on big sites like Monster or CareerBuilder. In fact, they probably don't have any official "intern" positions available. But that should not stop you. I recommend learning about these companies and (gasp!) calling them. That's right, call them and ask if they could use a hand from a bright and talented college student. You could even use some of the silly networking techniques I spoke about a few pages ago.

So how do you find these companies? There's no easy solution, but here are a few places to start:

Business Incubators
These are privately or government funded organizations that promote the growth of startups in and around your city. Almost any medium to large city has one. So if your one-horse-town doesn't, chances are, the closest metro does. Incubators provide funding, business consulting services, and sometimes inexpensive office space to get a startup off the ground.

Just search online for "business incubators" plus your

city. If that doesn't work, check your state's Department of Development as they may have links under a "business" or "entrepreneurship" heading. That may get you a list. Start making phone calls stating your interest in business incubators or local startup companies. If that doesn't work, ask about any state grants given to encourage entrepreneurship. A list of recent recipients of such grants could lead to some good companies. Keep trying and eventually, you'll get to the right place.

Local Venture Capital Firms

Venture capital firms (or VC's) are companies who invest in startups or growing companies. The money usually comes from the founders of the firm, wealthy individuals, larger corporations, or government entities. A VC's job is to investigate startups and determine which ones have the best shot at success. In return for the money, VC's own a percentage of the company. Again, doing a search for local "venture capital" companies can be a start.

Note: Though a particular VC may be local, sometimes the companies they invest in (known as their "portfolio companies") may be all over the globe. There's a good chance that many of their investments are nearby.

Your University

Many colleges have a dedicated department to cultivate and commercialize innovations that were developed on campus by faculty or other university researchers. Stanford is well known for a list companies that started on campus. (Perhaps you've heard of Google?) In many cases, the universities own a percentage of the company. Try searching your school's web site for "office of technology licensing" or "technology commercialization." They could point you in the right direction. Sometimes, they can refer you to incubators or VC's they work with. You never know unless you start talking to people.

Your Local Chamber of Commerce

Most cities have a thriving Chamber of Commerce, which is an association of businesses that help promote each other and the community. Most of their web sites have a list of member companies, professional organizations. Some even have job postings or internship opportunities. Just understand that not all of the Chamber companies are small businesses or startups – so don't be surprised if you see some Fortune 100 companies in the directory.

There's your list. Now go get 'em. As I said several times in this section, you can't get anywhere unless you start making phone calls or sending e-mails. The worst things they can say are: "Sorry, you got the wrong department," or "I really don't know how to help," or "No, we aren't interested in hiring interns." If so, thank them, ask them if they know of anyone else that can help, or move on to the next number. You've got nothing to lose but the chance to gain some real-world experience.

5

"You can't lose much if you don't have anything to lose."

A good friend of mine told me over a beer (OK, several) that he had the best job in the world. I asked him why and he said, "Because, Pawan, I get paid to do what I love and to hang out with my friends."

Maybe it was the late hour in the night, maybe it was the ambiance of the venue, or maybe it was the alcohol talking, but my friend's quote resonated with me to my very core. He stated in one sentence the very essence of this entire book. Over the years of his career, he became an expert in a field he is passionate about. Additionally, he has created a network of meaningful relationships with other professionals who help each other succeed. To have both – a job you love and good people to work with – seems like an increasingly elusive goal to achieve. Or is it?

AN EQUATION FOR SUCCESS

I believe success can be expressed in the following pseudo-mathematical "Success Equation":

Success = (Effort + Time) x Opportunities

I'm not about to define "Success," because that is unique to every individual. Some regard Success as making tons of money. To others, it is raising a healthy family. Whatever your definition of Success, I believe the above equation still applies. No matter what you want to achieve, you need to exert enough "Effort" towards your goal. Then you need to give enough "Time" (some call it patience) to let the fruits of your Effort come to bare. A healthy network of meaningful relationships is a major component of "Opportunities." The more people who know you, the more job openings, client referrals, or business ideas they could potentially send your direction. The result of your Effort and Time are multiplied by the number of Opportunities you have, thus increasing your "Success" – however you define it.

No wonder that your years in college are such a pivotal period in your development. You will find no other point in your life when the three elements of the Success Equation (Effort, Time and Opportunities) are at their maximum. As a student, you have no lack of energy to put forth any Effort required. You (hopefully) do not have major obligations to eat up your Time. Finally, simply attending college opens your mind to valuable knowledge and inspiring people that can lead to more Opportunities.

What is most amazing about your time in college is how little risk is involved.

Say you take an entire quarter or semester "off" to network with professionals in your community, start a business, intern at a company or take classes outside your major. Let's say at the end of your quarter/semester, you conclude it was a complete waste of your time. Though this conclusion is very unlikely, what would you have lost? A few months that you can make up in the summer?

However, the upsides are huge. Perhaps you get an internship that turns into a job opportunity when you graduate. Maybe you realize your current major isn't right for you, and find the right fit. Or maybe you realize you are on the right path, and you use your "time off" just to confirm it.

Any of these scenarios have benefits that more than outweigh the time you spent away from class. As a college student, you have very little to lose and so much to gain. So please realize this and make the best of it.

LIVE TO WORK OR WORK TO LIVE?

I'd like to talk a little about life (groan) at the risk of sounding like your parents (double groan).

I've made an assumption about you when writing this book. I've assumed that you want to find a fulfilling career that happens to provide the lifestyle you want, such as enough money, prestige and personal fulfillment. If so, you are someone who "Lives to Work."

There is another category of people who realize what they truly love won't give them the lifestyle they want. While they may not hate their day job, they know they "Work to Live."

Their true passion is typically a hobby or pastime.

I have friends who could scuba dive every day of the year, or spend hours photographing wild birds or surf all day long. However, they know that if their passion was their profession, they wouldn't afford a nice house or raise a loving family or even pay the electricity bill.

There's nothing wrong with being a member of either group as long as you are happy. In the past few chapters, I have used the words "career" and "passion" interchangeably. All the tips and advice I've given will certainly help you find both – but sometimes they may not be the same thing.

I encourage you to be introspective and find what makes you content. You may determine that what you love does not provide you the lifestyle you want. Here are some examples: What if your consulting job requires you to travel 5 days a week, yet you want to have six kids? What if you have dreams of owning a big house and a boat but want to be a social worker?

I know, I know. The thoughts of raising a family or owning a house are too far out. I can appreciate that. All the more reason to explore your career options in college so you can determine if it syncs with the lifestyle you may want years from now.

FINAL THOUGHTS

Be fortunate we live in a country that embraces capitalism. Be relieved that we have a society that rewards hard work and initiative. Be thankful for the vast opportunities available to all of us.

I hope you find your passions in life. I hope your professional career is as rewarding as possible. I also hope that once you are in your profession, you take time to mentor students with your experience and knowledge. Tell them that their time in college is like a race to the starting line and the road beyond is filled with opportunities for success.

Best of luck to you.

Recommended Reading

The following are books of all genres that influenced the way I think, my career or my outlook on society. I hope they inspire you in the same way.

Allen, David. *Getting Things Done*. New York: Penguin, 2002.

Many successful people I know have way too many things on their minds. David Allen describes a seemingly obvious exercise to free your mind of such stress: write them all down! The problem is, few of us do this regularly since we don't carry around a pen and paper. In addition to writing our to-do list, Mr. Allen provides a very easy system to make sure we accomplish as much as we can in a given day.

Andrusia, David and Rick Haskins. *Brand Yourself: How to Create an Identity for a Brilliant Career.* New York: Ballantine Books, 2000.

Brand Yourself was the inspiration to the four steps I describe to find your passion. David Andrusia and Rick Haskins wants you to think about your name, image and reputation the same way marketers think about well known brands. In one chapter he asks you to turn your skills into benefits. Crest toothpaste has the *skill* of containing sodium fluoride. But that is not what is on the box. The *benefit* of containing sodium fluoride is that it "fights cavities," which is repeated many times on the box and in ads. The authors encourage you to do the same with your skills.

Clarke, Arthur C. and Stephen Baxter. *The Light of Other Days.* New York: Voyager, 2002.

This book has nothing to do with business at all, but

it's my all time favorite book, period. Arthur C. Clarke has an uncanny talent to forecast the way society will be impacted by technological advances. In this book, he talks about how new wormhole technology becomes common place and allows anyone to see what anyone else is doing. Though society is upended due to complete lack of privacy, a new era of truth is established. Fascinating book – even for those who don't read sci-fi.

Greene, Robert. *48 Laws of Power.* New York: Penguin, 2000.

I certainly don't abide by every law that Robert Green writes about, but I do take a few to heart. Like "Law 5: Guard your reputation with your life, your success depends on it." *48 Laws of Power* is a mixture of the philosophies of Machiavelli, Sun-tzu (The Art of War), Carl von Clausewitz and others.

Johnson, Spencer. *Who Moved My Cheese?: An Amazing Way to Deal with Change in Your Work and in Your Life.* G. P. Putnam's Sons: 1998.

Though the metaphor seems childish, Spencer Johnson

makes several in-your-face points: stop whining, take responsibility over your actions, and work towards your goals.

Kawasaki, Guy and Michele Moreno. *Rules for Revolutionaries*. New York: HarperBusiness, 1999.

I've always admired Guy Kawasaki after seeing him speak several times. My favorite line from this book is "Don't worry, be crappy." He reminds us to not get caught up with the details the first time we do anything. Whether it's starting a company, learning to cook, or writing a book, just do it and improve later. Great advice for perfectionists like me.

About the Author

Pawan (pronounced like "oven" with a "p") Murthy is a serial entrepreneur and public speaker. He also claims to be a marketing expert since he doesn't believe there's enough evidence to refute that statement. Pawan is passionate about building things, telling stories and helping others find their passions. He lives with his family in Columbus, OH.

To learn more about Pawan, please visit:
www.PawanMurthy.com
www.linkedin.com/in/pmurthy